Blue Honey

poems

Beth Copeland

The Broadkill River Press
Milton, Delaware

Blue Honey
© Beth Copeland 2017

Library of Congress Control Number:
2017954227
ISBN 978-1-940120-76-8

The Broadkill River Press
P.O. Box 63,
Milton, DE 19968
the_broadkill_press@earthlink.net
www.thebroadkillriverpress.com/

front cover photograph by
Rebecca Copeland

In loving memory of my parents,

E. Luther Copeland and Louise Tadlock Copeland

Acknowledgments

Acknowledgment is made to the following publications for poems (or earlier versions of poems) that originally appeared in them:

Aeolian Harp, America is Not the World: A Pankhearst Collection, Atlanta Review, Bay Leaves, Caesura, Charlotte Viewpoint, For Seniors Only, Iodine Poetry Journal, Kakalak, Mockingheart Review, Naugatuck River Review, New Millennium Writings, Peacock Journal, Pinesong, Pirene's Fountain: Skin Deep, Poetry in Plain Sight, Poet's Market, Quill Ink, Rattle, Shining Rock Poetry Anthology, The Southern Poetry Anthology: Volume VII: North Carolina, Tar River Poetry, Twelve Point Collective, Weatherings: A Good Works Project, and *The Wide Shore: A Journal of Global Women's Poetry.*

I am grateful to Roger Weingarten for guiding me as I revised these poems and for his gift of the title "Premature Elegy."

Thank you to Addy McCulloch and Cheryl Whitehead for critiquing some of the poems as they emerged.

I wrote and revised many of the poems during a residency at Weymouth Center. Thank you to the Friends of Weymouth for providing me with a private room in a peaceful setting where I could write.

In loving memory of my parents,

E. Luther Copeland and Louise Tadlock Copeland

Acknowledgments

Acknowledgment is made to the following publications for poems (or earlier versions of poems) that originally appeared in them:

Aeolian Harp, America is Not the World: A Pankhearst Collection, Atlanta Review, Bay Leaves, Caesura, Charlotte Viewpoint, For Seniors Only, Iodine Poetry Journal, Kakalak, Mockingheart Review, Naugatuck River Review, New Millennium Writings, Peacock Journal, Pinesong, Pirene's Fountain: Skin Deep, Poetry in Plain Sight, Poet's Market, Quill Ink, Rattle, Shining Rock Poetry Anthology, The Southern Poetry Anthology: Volume VII: North Carolina, Tar River Poetry, Twelve Point Collective, Weatherings: A Good Works Project, and *The Wide Shore: A Journal of Global Women's Poetry.*

I am grateful to Roger Weingarten for guiding me as I revised these poems and for his gift of the title "Premature Elegy."

Thank you to Addy McCulloch and Cheryl Whitehead for critiquing some of the poems as they emerged.

I wrote and revised many of the poems during a residency at Weymouth Center. Thank you to the Friends of Weymouth for providing me with a private room in a peaceful setting where I could write.

Blue Honey

Contents

I

II

III

I

Remember how to forget.
—Edwin Honig

Good Intentions

It's not the bee's fault, Daddy says, pulling
the stinger

from the tender flesh of my inner arm. *Look,
it's dead. It didn't*

mean any harm. The honeybee,
no bigger than a pumpkin

seed in his palm, its striped
torso of topaz

and gold like a Phoenician
bead. But I didn't mean

to kill it. I didn't
even see it until

it stung. Bees hover
above dandelion

suns and buzz from purple clover
to hive. I will love

and be loved, sting and be
stung. No one

gets out
alive.

Sign: *SLOW*

Death in Family. How will slowing
help the people in the white
clapboard farmhouse grieve, or Daddy,

unable to eat solid food, a line
of drool dangling from his lip? Will

a lighter touch on the pedal ease
Mother's journey, hospitalized
with a broken hip, unable to recollect her best

friend's name when I pass the phone? I want
to spare my vanishing

parents the indignity of lingering, so
please forgive me if I burn
rubber past the farmhouse.

Water into Wine

My octogenarian Baptist parents wouldn't
know Rothschild from rotgut but love a little

vino before bed. She sips a thimble
sized cup and titters, *I'm tipsy,* while he

bellows, *Bottom's up!* and chugs
Two Buck Chuck. She hides

her illicit cache in the cupboard beneath
the steel sink. What if church

members drop by and spy Richard's Wild
Irish Rose, Ripple, or Pagan

Pink? After supper, they recline
in matching velour Lazy-Boys, lost

in *Matlock* and *Dynasty*, drowsy
with dreams of mountain

streams and jugs of sweet
muscadine.

Featherweight Singer

My mother ferried her sewing machine
across the Pacific four times, stitching

continents as if
they were linen scraps—America

to Asia, Asia to America—following
Daddy as he exchanged his

version of heaven
for a suitcase of Shinto

scrolls. I fell
asleep to the white noise of that

black machine, to the song of steady
seams like wind in cottonwoods

or rain on rafters, to my mother's breathing
when I climbed her bed after bad dreams.

My sisters and I wore our Sunday best—puffed
sleeves, gathered skirts, and sashes

sewn on the Featherweight Singer as we slept.
When I was fourteen, she tried to teach me

to pin Simplicity patterns to fabric and cut
on printed lines, but I—sullen

and careless, too young
to believe I'd ever be alone—

thought she'd never leave. On her old
machine, I sew silk

infinity scarves for sisters
and friends from vintage Varanasi

saris, listening to my
mother's song in the rise

and fall of the needle and *World without
end*—whir of the unwinding

spool—*amen, amen.*

The Dime-Store Mirror

tilted in lamplight
reflects stars and the pale
moon of her face. Am I
the child in her eye? Am I
getting smaller, or does the horizon
lift as fog rises on mountains, blue
at the root of flames?
She stares at the vanishing
point of sky and sea. I don't
know what's me, her, or if
we're still moored
by flesh. Her breath
clouds its surface as she
lipsticks Rapture
Red and powders her cheeks.

Hinged, it opens, so I

can powder and slick
on Fire and Ice. My breath
clouds its surface. No longer
moored by flesh, I still don't
know what's me, her, or if
she stares at the vanishing
seam between sky and sea.
As fog rises on blue
mountains in its
oval frame, the horizon
shifts as I shrink. Am I still
the child in her eye
where the moon
of my mother's face reflects
stars tilted in twilight?

14

Mnemosyne's

acrostic: a future more dreaded than death: Alzheimer's
    and memory

locked in limbo between thought and limbic
    flow, in a fading

zone with erased address and area code, notes scrawled
    on envelopes as reminders to

his mind's failing GPS, missed appointments, smoke
    detectors set off, and

early morning ramblings into traffic without a map
    to get home.

It creeps along like a time-lapsed peony's
    decay, just

minor evaporations of breath
    and objects misplaced—

eyeglasses microwaved, car keys stashed in the medicine cabinet,
    a cell phone

refrigerated—followed by moody confusion, difficulty
    reading or following recipes, losing track of changing

seasons.

Denial: who
    wants to accept

it? Family
         insists it's just

senior
         moments, no matter, but

eventually,
         months

at sea without
         a compass or

sail to get from
         A to

eternity.

Daddy Dreams He Misses the Boat

I'm late. The ship's sailing without me,
Daddy, age 91, informs my mother
over oatmeal. *Only a dream,*

she sighs as she butters his toast, *only
a dream,* until he slumps
into his coffee mug. A tall

young man traveling to Yokohama
with my dark-haired mother, a Bible
in his hand and a baby in the crook

of his arm. Three times
he made that voyage, then from the sky,
looking down at white-capped

clouds like waves that broke
against the *President Wilson*'s deck.
A brass paperweight of that ship

used to anchor his desk. When I ask
where it went, he blinks as if
returning from another

hemisphere into daylight, still
adrift between this continent
and the next.

Falling Lessons

Because of neuropathy his feet no longer
feel the floor as he steps into a field of lost

sensation, falling in the shower, bruised
but bones unbroken, falling as he pours

sunflower seeds into the bird feeder: blood
from his head spurts onto brick; falling

at the nursing home where a yellow Falling Star
sign taped to his door reminds

staff he's a frequent faller who needs an arm
to walk from his bed to the john in the Memory

Garden, where the memory
impaired wander. Once he dreamed

my sister fell from a second
story railing. His recollection

of her childhood
accident has become a reel

of remembered dreams filtered
through what he believes

is real. My memory
of him changes as he loses his. Has he

forgotten flesh and blood, his seawater
eyed child, his Scots-Irish

stock—forgotten he'll fall if he tries
to walk his memory of those

he loves still outside the fog
that will slowly cover us when

we wonder what we forgot to ask
before he lost his words—last

snow falling when he almost
drove off the road on our way to the Blue

Ridge mountains or why we wanted to
go there? Dizzy after blood tests, I tell him

how lucky I feel after fainting
at the doctor's. I close

my eyes to blind myself
to the red cord running

to the vial, but I feel it
flow from a childhood

tetanus shot. When I stand
to leave, all the life

drains. *Daddy, I must've
taken falling lessons from you*, I tell him, slumped

and brooding in his wheelchair. *Like you, I fell
but didn't break.* Sad

he can't answer, I wonder if he's proud
of being such a tough

old bird, of the spatters from his latest
mishap or if he wonders what I'm prattling

about, sad as I kiss his cheek, say goodbye, and disembark
into a memory in the making,

wondering if I'll lose
my father funneling into a freeze

frame rush in my ears—the flurry of furious
wings as I fall.

Falling Lessons: Erasure & Variation

He swoops, hawk-eyed,
into my watery day
dream of flotsam—

railings of bones, serpentine
roads, fields, fog,
a peacock

eyed child who almost
forgot that vein of sorrow
in snow. Herons

brood over blue
mountains where his
Scots-Irish forebears planted

holy hell among Joe
Pye Weed and hollyhocks. I step
into the frieze of my

father stepping
into flames.

Acrophobic

Not a fear of falling, she whispers
through gritted teeth, hands white
knuckling the steering wheel as we drive
through a downpour across the bridge. Below
the Savannah swells like mercury beneath

steel spanning Georgia to South Carolina.

Not afraid, she sighs, when we reach
the other side, *of being pushed
or losing my balance. Afraid
that when I'm standing on the edge I might
look down and jump.*

Escape Artist

No one believed the old man
would escape with a Wanderguard
strapped to his wrist like Houdini's

handcuffs. Hunched
at the glass door, from beneath
hooded eyelids he watches

nurses punch codes to lift
the latch. Once
they found him at a gas station

across the street in a wheelchair, waving
as they wheeled him back. A janitor
found him on a landing

after he pulled himself down
a steep flight. The staff call
his escapes elopements, as if

he's running off with a bride
instead of leaving a locked
Alzheimer's wing. He believes

Mother and I sleep in the room
next door and the nursing home's a hotel.
A master of the art of escape, he left her

to cross the ocean with four little girls while he
took a whirlwind trip around the globe, sending
postcards from Singapore,

Jordan, Switzerland, and a green taffeta
dress from Paris she never wore. Watch
him escape from this riveted trunk, breaking

chains, unlocking all locks, that sneaky
sweet old son of a fox.

Dial M for Memory

My 87-year-old mother calls
twice today because she forgot
she already called me. *Just calling to
say I'm still alive and kicking*, she says

twice because she forgot
this morning's communiqué. *Called to
tell you my clock's still ticking*, she says
when I lift the phone from its cradle, which

she said this morning. I fall
into a trance as she unveils the same story
when I answer, which is what
drives me to drink zombies: she puts me

in a trance with the same inventory
ad infinitum. I love my mother, who drives
me to the brink, putting me
into a Möbius loop, like a *Groundhog Day*

moment, *ad infinitum*. I love her, but
conversations turned into hula hoops
are what I dread; like *Groundhog Day*'s Phil
the weatherman, I want to talk to her

but dread conversations that burn
into my brain like grooves on vinyl. I want
to talk to her, but I want
to hang up, too, after listening to her

refrain like grooves on vinyl. It's not her
fault she's forgetful. I dance
the hang-up/keep-talking tango
of my mother's questions. It's not her

fault she's forgetful! When
my mother calls, I tap dance
to her questions before she blurts,
I just called to say I love you.

Chicken Dance

Daddy rips paper emblazoned with red
and blue balloons, lifts the lid—

a robin's egg
blue polo nestled

in tissue. Unimpressed, he tears
the envelope and gawks

at a dancing rooster: WHY
DID THE CHICKEN

CROSS THE ROAD?—opens
the yellow card to the *oom*

pah pah of a polka—TO WISH YOU
A HAPPY BIRTHDAY!—shuts

it, opens it—*oom pah
pah*—and shuts it. Slowly,

he shreds the rooster's red
comb with his finger

nails; feathers fly
like question marks

from its shaking
tail. In his quest for the source,

he breaks the tiny brass
mechanism glued

inside the bird's
breast where music began

with a turning page
then stopped.

Nothing Blue

When I leave she asks, *Are you
going to that cabin with Phil?* She can't

recall our wedding. She wore
a periwinkle dress she bought at Belk's

so she wouldn't
embarrass me garbed in something

old as she sipped champagne and nibbled
cake. *Yes, I live there. We're*

married, remember? She blinks. *Oh,
that's right.* Not her fault, but I'm so

tired of wanting
her to hold onto that

one day. When I arrive to chauffeur
her to the doctor, she's not

dressed but tells the nurse, *I could live
on my own if I had a family.* What

am I, chopped
liver? She tells her friends I never

visit because she forgets. On the drive
home, I pass a blur of chicory

growing wild around
a crinoline of Queen Anne's

Lace—something
old, nothing

new, one thing borrowed,
almost blue.

Last Word

From my purse I fish photos as a distraction
from Daddy's silence, pointing to a plaque

we bought on our honeymoon—*Welcome
to our Cabin*—a porch swing,

two rocking chairs. *See, I painted them
red because we needed a pop*

of color. I search his face
for a flicker of interest. Another

snapshot: a raccoon
dangling from eaves steals

seeds from a feeder. *Daddy, look
at that rascal!* He doesn't

laugh. I turn
over a snapshot of the moon

deck where Phil and I talk over wine
at sunset, watching bats

sail across the persimmon sky, then the cracked
ends of firewood hoarded

under a blue tarp. Nothing. Next, a rough
hewn mantle above the brick

hearth, the punched-tin chandelier
over the three-plank table, Blue

Willow platters stacked in the hutch. With
a trembling finger, he points

behind the bright swing to a window
frame's peeling paint so

weathered it's almost dark
as the cabin logs. Haltingly,

he mumbles, *red.*

There

Snapped string,
pearls scattered.

For her, each
synapse is a pearl,

unstrung. Always
surprised, she's

happy as if
I arrived in a blink—a moment

lapsed, finding the lost
bead of my story newly

spun, an orient
orb from the ocean floor. I kiss

her cheek, touch
her hair, so

ghostly it lights
the darkened room. When

I leave, she'll forget
I was ever there.

Hymn

Daddy no longer
speaks but sings old
hymns when a friend hammers
the piano. *O*
bear me away on your snow
white wings. He can't

ask for things he needs—a hand
kerchief, extra pillow, or lost
hearing aid—but sings
note for note,
each hymn
by

heart. Music
brings back melodies
memorized
long ago. *Bear me away*
on your snow-white
wings. He sings

his childhood faith,
mornings in the mountains,
oaks, creeks, and birds. *O*
Come angel band. Can't
speak but sings. *Come*
and around me

stand rings through sage
green nursing home halls
like an echo. O
his baritone! *On your snow*
white wings to my
immortal

home springs from silence
like a stream from stones
below. Daddy no longer
speaks but sings *O bear me*
away on your snow
white wings.

Kintsugi

Mother's Japanese friends
send cards she forgets

to open—prints of blond
birds flying

over turquoise waves, pine branches
burdened with snow. Her mailbox,

stuffed with letters
and junk. I slice

into an envelope and pluck a handwritten
note from Kinko-san: *I have not heard*

from you. I am worried. You are so
old. Mother snorts, *She's*

almost as old as I am!
and we laugh

at what's lost
in translation. She forgets bills,

to brush her teeth or swallow
her thyroid pills and Lipitor

but remembers Kinko-san
from long ago. Should I write to say you're

okay? *I'll do it
later,* but she won't. She stares

at a maple for hours when I'm
not here, her hair a corona

of uncombed
dandelion seeds. Should I

laugh or cry? Like a broken
bowl mended with molten

gold, she's more
beautiful than before. I hold

her in the heart
of my heart

where she's whole.

Keeping Time

In the blue wheelchair, his eyes
open when I enter. Does

he know me? Maybe
he dives into the resemblance

to a snapshot
pinned to his wall. At 94,

he drifts in and out of distant time
zones and forgotten memories. We graze

National Geographic, snowflakes, maple
leaves, and stars magnified

thousands of degrees. The clock
doesn't advise

me to stay or leave, his watch
somewhere still keeping time. When

I was small, I'd hop onto his lap
while he held it to my ear, the gold

warm from his wrist. As I
listened to its ticking, I believed

he could hold back
time forever, a pulse that

would never stop.

Sunrise: Lunch

Embarrassed when Mother
introduces me twice to the Sunrise
ladies, asking, *Have you met Beth?*
I nudge her and whisper, *It's okay,*
they know. Until blurry eyes look up
through bifocals and ask, *Who*

the dickens are you? Who
am I? I glance at my prim, proper mom
sipping sweet tea with lemon, cutting up
quiche and mouth-sized bites of sunrise
colored melon. *Lady Gaga,* I say. *Okay!*
the bleary-eyed woman blurts. *Beth,*

have you met Mrs. Mabry? This is Beth.
I nod to her hunched, shrunken pal who
extends a liver-spotted claw. *I'm Kay.*
A trout-limp shake, unlike Mother's
firm grasp. Arthritic, I surmise
and don't squeeze. Turning my cup

over for coffee, I pass the ketchup
to henna-haired Harriet. *This—is Beth!*
Dear God, give me a Tequila Sunrise
and double shot of patience, please! *Who?*
Harriet asks. *My daughter,* Mother
huffs. Harriet squeezes ketchup. Okie

dokie. Heinz squirts, farts. O Fucking K.
How are you? I ask. Instead of looking up
Harriet chomps a pickle while another
chum, plump and short of breath,
picks at a chicken breast and gasps, *Who's
your guest?* almost as surprised

as if she'd seen the Lord's son rise
from the dead. *You okay?*
I ask as the incredulous woman—whose
wristband says Alice McRae—hacks up
half a lung. Mother whispers, *Beth,
she coughs to get attention.* Mother's

Sunrise friends grip their walkers, pull themselves
up and shuffle off. *This is my daughter, Beth,*
Mother yoo-hoos. Kay, like a barn owl, asks, *Who?*

Feeding Daddy at 95

Big appetite, second helpings, Mother always
served him first. What's

on his tray is pureed: meat, potatoes,
cabbage, squash—even bread—mashed

into a pulp, and sweet tea thickened
with gelatin. He's forgetting how

to swallow, so I slowly
launch one spoonful and pause

before the next. When I
was small he'd pretend the spoon

was a zooming airplane. Sometimes
I balked and zippered

my lips if he wanted to land liver or limas
onto my tongue, but sometimes I'd laugh

and he'd dive that plane
into my maw! I'd gulp, amused,

but tricked. His napkin's tucked into his shirt
like a bib; with his bald head and beak-like nose, he's

a baby bird opening
for a worm as he leans to

meet the airplane bearing applesauce
and ice cream for dessert.

Requiem with White Roses

Five for her kids, six
for her grandchildren, one

for Charlotte, her great
granddaughter. I place her Mother's

Day bouquet in water, conjuring a ghost
rose in florist ferns pinned

to her dress with a pearl
tipped hat pin. White

meant an orphan, her mother,
Grace, dead before

my delivery. Sisters and I wore rosebud
corsages like lipstick or wounds

on our collars to honor our living
mother, whose table won't

always be set with
silver and a blue Arita vase. I place

my palm
on her sloped

shoulder and silently swear
that someday I'll pin an ivory

rose to my lapel or slide
its stem into water

and aspirin to prolong
its life as petals drop

slowly onto my lace
tablecloth.

Fugue

Fog gauzes fragments
of a dream. Is this

how you felt when words
like schools of fish blurred

on the page, you, who read
Japanese and penned

crosswords in ballpoint? Your fate
settled on your shoulders so

silently no one
noticed. *Let go,*

a friend says, *Don't
fight,* but I hold

fast against forgetting
the road where you stopped

for coffee
ice cream that tasted of the perked

Luzianne you spooned into my milk
if I begged. I licked the melting toffee

colored cone until I dozed,
hypnotized by the radio, believing

I was safe as you rounded
curves, then carried me upstairs.

Like a pearl behind white
clouds, the morning

sun could be the moon. Is this
the late afternoon road I travel

every day? Did I veer
into white poppies or dream

I was driving instead of driving
home?

Twilight

In what Steinbeck calls *the hour*
of the pearl—the interval between day

and night—we wait for this
world to turn while the sun

sinks behind black
pines. I raise

a glass of pinot, a bouquet
of pears, mangoes,

and tangerines swirled
in pale gold. *I wish they'd*

die. You don't
answer, but I know you

hear me. Daddy, trapped
in dementia's limbo; Mother,

in the land of memory
loss. I love them but want

the blade to drop, for the bleeding
to stop, the sky

the color of a Tahitian
pearl, a blend of pewter

and slate. I sip my wine. One gold
poplar leaf spirals

from the tree, landing
like a gift from above in your lap. Gradually,

they're leaving us, and we dread the long
goodbye, the anticipatory

grief before they go, wondering if
there's another room beyond

the one I visit every
other week.

Dear Omniscient Narrator

Please don't
let me linger

in the ellipses
of dementia and disease

murmuring goodbye again
and again to family and friends.

Write a simple sentence with a period at the end.

II

*All you pray for at this age is a peaceful
hour in which to change worlds.*
—E. Luther Copeland

Release

Imagine a goldfinch
in your fist. Open it

as olive wings soar
over dark steeples. If

you're grieving for what
never was or will be, bring

your fingers
to your palm, always

empty, the finch
already free.

What I Remember When He Dies

My sister calls it *a spanking* but
it wasn't. He yanked

my ankles, held me
upside-down and slapped

me like a midwife
forces a newborn baby

to breathe, but I was nine, listening
to my sisters plead, *Stop,*

Daddy, please. He dropped me.
I ran to my room, sobbing.

How could he? people ask.
What could a child

do to deserve such a beating? But being
battered was better than being told what

a bad girl I was, so
selfish, so ugly, so un

Christian, that the brunt
of his palm on my butt

was a blessing because it meant
his sin was greater

than mine and I
had been forgiven.

Exhale

The hospice nurse says he's
transitioning. I tell
my students to work transitional
words into their sentences to lead
the reader from one idea to the next,
but slipping from life into death isn't
as simple as revising a passage by adding
first, then, next. First,

he lies in bed with his mouth open
while Mother holds
his hand and my brother swabs
his lips with lemon-flavored
gel. Then he takes another
breath and next, exhales, flying
from one
continent to the other.

Memory Book

Nothing written: *Where*

> *snow falls, children make wings*

appointments, dates, kids'

> *like cherubs flying to the sky's blue*

birthdays, friends, and craftsmen to repair

> *cathedral windows and assemble a woman from*

bones, wires, pipe, and crumbling

> *snow, dressing her in*

plaster. I keep forgetting to write on these

> *my ratty old brassiere!*

blank pages. What good's this stupid book if

> *I make snow cream for the children*

I can't remember what happened yesterday?

> *with vanilla, sugar, and milk*

Where's my husband? Did he die? Was it

> *stirred with spoonfuls of snow. Was it*

raining when we buried him? Tears ran down my cheeks

when I watched a woman melt

like invisible ink

on melting snow.

Grief

We cut down the dead
pine next to the cabin. Alive,

it loomed above shingled roof
and power lines as

he, lumberjack
strong at 6 foot 3, once

towered over me. As a boy,
he sold huckleberries, wild

ginseng, and spoke
to God in a chapel of sycamores

and oaks. At 18, he rolled
and loaded logs from steep

mountain skids onto a two-ton
International, swerving

off a curve when he fell
asleep at the wheel

near Summersville. When I
was a child, he spoke

sacred names—beech, poplar,
hickory—on an afternoon as crisp

as sliced apples, and slanting light
shone gold through yellow gills

of the gingko. I dropped
leaves into a brown Winn-Dixie

bag—a redbud like a valentine
and a scarlet, star

shaped sweet gum leaf pressed
between wax

paper sheets and flame. When I
was in college, he read *Foxfire*

books and built a cabin from fallen
pines. He climbed a chain

link fence at 80 to chop
wood for the poor, hungry

for the haft of an ax. The nursing
home intake worker asked

his profession. *I worked*
in the woods, he said, his Yale

PhD, years in pulpits
and classrooms, pages

he wrote like withered leaves falling
from trees that sheltered him. Now

under a constellation-lit sky, I turn into the glow
of the gravel drive, pulling up to

an unfamiliar home—nothing but sawdust,
a stump, and a hole where that

pine once stood.

Premature Elegy

She fears drowning most because she can't
even dog paddle, watching from the shore

as her kids crawl farther
and farther from view, knowing

there's nothing she can do. As her lungs
fill with fluid, is there nothing

I can do as she backfloats
the electric bed? While the heart

monitor charts her tides, the baby
faced doctor drains

her lungs but rivers
empty into a fan-shaped

estuary that flows into the ocean
within her heart as she drifts away.

Pretty

The doctor says, *You must*
have been beautiful when you

were young. Mother
struggles to lift

her head, hair mussed in a titmouse
tuft from the pillow, her cheeks—once milky

as magnolia petals—speckled
with age, but the wide-set

brown eyes and high cheekbones
people compared to Jackie

Kennedy's still shine through.
At ten, I paused before

the mirror, removed my cat's
eye glasses, astigmatism

softening angles, round
cheeks rosy from pedaling

my Schwinn against
the wind, sprigs of hair

like sun spokes sprung
from my ponytail's elastic

band, eyes a blur of sage
ringed with smoke. Mama

fried okra while Becky scribbled
in a Sleeping Beauty coloring book

and baby Luke crawled
after a tennis ball. *Mama, am I*

pretty? She flipped a cornmeal
crusted pod with a fork. *You'll never*

be a great beauty. Crisco sizzled
and spat in the skillet. *But you're pleasing*

enough. My fantasy
of strutting down a runway

with an armful of long-stemmed
roses as Bert crooned, *There*

she is—Miss
America, shattered like a Coke

bottle on concrete. I checked
the mirror again, this time

in my glasses—I was plain,
with Daddy's aquiline

nose and pinched
lips, with darkening

hair she called *dishwater*
blonde. A good Christian

woman wasn't supposed to think
too highly of herself or—God

forbid—be vain. I was supposed
to be modest like Mama or brave

like Lottie Moon, the missionary
who starved to save Chinese children

for Jesus. Now I smooth
her wild hair, so

sparse you can see her scalp. *Yes,*
I tell the clipboard

clutching doctor, my eyes locked
on his. *My mother was. She still is.*

Crane Wife

She told a nurse, *I'm leaving soon*
to live with my husband. I won't

be coming back. Days later,
the ER doctor isn't sure

if she's had a stroke
but I know

something's wrong. She tries
to speak but can only

moan and yank at the breathing
mask, glaring at me. She wants

to follow him to a new
country as she crossed

the ocean to Japan, believing
God had called him to serve, she

to serve him. I call
my sisters and brother. They book

flights, while at her
bedside, I recall my first

flight when I was five, Japanese
friends waving handkerchiefs.

I lugged a straw
bag of treasures: a small

brocade purse with ivory dog
tooth clasp, Chi-Chi the stuffed

monkey, a book of fairy tales turned
to the page where the crane

wife flies away on white
wings. Chi-Chi forgotten

on the plane, I cried, clinging
to her skirt as she

sprinted through airports
with three little girls and a newborn

in a basket. *What if we can't find
Daddy?* America looked huge

on the globe. We woke
in Alaska. Passengers

swaddled in blankets burst
outside, laughing, but she

wouldn't let us, so we peered
through oval windows

at falling snow. I hold
her hand, the skin

thin as rice paper,
and whisper, *It's okay, Momma.*

You can go.

Her Hand

always smelled like Jergen's. When I
was sick, she'd place a palm

on my forehead to calm
fever's pitch and ocean waves

of nausea. Now I place
mine on her brow, while beeping

monitors chart the peaks
and planes of her heart—I stroke

her gnarled fingers, skin
so thin you could shine

a light to the other side, morphine
drip taped where veins divide into bruised

tributaries of tattoo blue. I squeeze
it. She's gone.

Lost Rings

Maybe her hand refused
to relinquish its gold

worn thin as a prayer over 66 years
of loving him. Maybe someone

stole her rings before
she was moved from hospital

to morgue or maybe
the mortician didn't

notice them as he pushed
her frail body into the concrete

chamber. Are we breathing
her gold and carbon

dust? Is her diamond
falling as we lower her urn

into soil? Does she look down,
amused that we mourn

the loss of rings that cost
so little, a chip

of stone, mere tokens
of what they shared. When he stopped

to clear the Plymouth's
windshield, his wedding band slipped

from his finger. He couldn't
find it on the road. The next day,

he drove back—there
it was!—in a stream

of melted snow, scratched
by the plow and tire

chains. He'd run
his thumb

over nicks as he told
the story of what

he'd lost and found
until the rough

spots were worn smooth
as water.

Midwinter Grave

A freight train rumbles over a dark
trestle—far away flakes fall

fast into the haloed
locomotive headlamp, the low

note of a warning
whistle heralds

her absence. A honey
lozenge like sunlight retrieved

from the bottom of my purse melts
on my tongue. I blow

on my fingertips'
memory

of Shalimar's amber
scent I'd dab

behind my earlobes
and in my throat's

hollow from the bottle
on her maple dresser that floats

on the wind through oaks. Slipping
off my gloves, I trace

letters chiseled in granite. Ashes,
her December

hair. Snow.

Crossing

A yearling waits. I slow down, then stop,
as five fawns step from fog, each
smaller than the other. I picture

my sisters and brother pairing
up for the holidays without
me. What held us

together is gone. After
she died, Becky flew to Mexico to swim
with whales. Joy

pawed through Mother's
clothes for socks or pantyhose.
Judy ransacked random

scraps in her files for secret
codes. Luke closed
her checking account. This

morning my eye trails the fawns'
safe passage into the grove: *Where's
the mother?*

Concrete Angel

Becky plants a red silk rose
in the fold of the angel's robe

and shoots a rain
scarred cheek and archaic smile

against Grandfather Mountain,
cedars and a cyclone

fence with strand of barbwire
like greenbrier thorns. I snap

headstones splotched
with lichen and stark

granite markers in the grass—*Mother,*
Father, and a molar-white

stone with *Ba* chiseled
on a broken half. Whose

baby sleeps beneath that severed
word? Whose loved ones

rest in this small mountain
graveyard where bones

crumble to nothing? *Who*
will grieve for us?

III

An angel has no memory.
—Terry Southern

Shinto Scroll

Red-crowned cranes in delicate
brush strokes on silk

between a gray
and gold brocade

border. An almost invisible
white, they pause on Hokkaido

snow before a hyacinth
blue lake. One, tall

on long legs; the smaller one's
bill tucked into a black

tipped wing. Symbolic
of longevity and love

that weathers time
and cold, they will never fly,

folded wings caught
on an antique bolt

I roll into my suitcase
before I leave.

Weymouth Morning

for James Autio

Wake to birdsong breaking the night's
silence—yellow
warblers, cardinals,

and vireos' coded notes in the key
of C and sunrise as faux
birds of styrofoam

and feathers float from fish line
on a mobile of immobile, flightless ruby
eyed doves, pink

wrens and peach
plumed sparrows. Yesterday,
mute to the calls of birds, I tried

to write, but
like a paper crane on strings, I ran
wounded and silent,

my fingertips over the black
cover of my notebook where
a friend painted a crow, touching

brush strokes of smoke
whorled wings. Daybreak
opens another

blank page. I place
my pen in the notch between
thumb and forefinger

as the mockingbird sings.

Onions

She chopped uncut bulbs like shrunken skulls
dug from dirt, shrink-wrapped in brittle

skins on a pig-shaped
cutting board's pine

knot eye as she stared through steam
at white camellias

beyond the fence, dabbing
her brown eyes with the hem

of a gingham apron. While I slice
through this season's layer of grief

and peel away another
onion within

the onion—Mother won't
glimpse flamingo

pink azaleas or rain
drenched Rowdy

Red tomatoes or maples
bleed and blaze. My bones

relive the morning
we lowered her

through falling snow. I pull rings
from rings, wondering when

I'll reach the pearl
white bud at the core

where the girl within
weeps.

Cleave

As I leave, I want you
to light a candle in memory's
alcove where my face is haloed

instead of harboring that florid
flashback of me smashing
a wine glass on tiles

when you said you weren't
going with me to counseling. I drank
myself into shadows

and wailed for years of giving you
everything I had—for what? Fist
pounding on granite,

I begged you
to hit me so even
strangers could see

you hurt me—writing
letters to ex-lovers, even
refusing to drive when the doctor

dilated my eyes, not
chauffeuring me to the hospital when
Mother was dying. When that

glass shattered, I thought, *This
is how it feels.* I wanted
you to say, *Don't*

go, remembering marigolds
and seafoam roses you left
on my desk—nights we bruised

petals you'd strewn across
our bed. Is this pairing of pain
and passion the moon's

push-pull, the longing to keep
our lives tethered as tides
return and retreat, as

we cleave together,
cleave apart?

Carolina Monsoon

Rain without
you falls

from eaves filled
with moss. You're

gone but
called to ask if

I was driving. *I'm so
worried.* I'm

okay. *Aren't you
with Phil?* I'm

not. *Oh,
I forgot.*

Rain falls
in sheets from

gutters stuffed
with brown,

soggy leaves. Before
you died, I

lived through
a storm. It's

raining, Mother. I'm
homeless,

alone. *You're married
on the moon.*

That tarnished silver
summer where an empty

nest reminds me you
died under longleaf

pines. You
said, *Don't*

*you
live outside?* No,

in a cabin. Don't you
remember? *Now I*

*know where
you sleep.*

Fledglings

A wren weaves a nest on a wreath
of burlap and sweet gum

burrs, bearing twigs, pine straw,
and leaves back and forth

while you and I, my dearest, rock
on the porch, listening to *Idiot Wind*

between citronella torches lit
to ward off mosquitoes. We keep

as much distance as we can, but
the nest's too

close to the creaking screen door as we
come and go. Months before, I left

for a furnished Fayetteville
studio, lugging books, sweaters

and shoes from rooms I'd
scrubbed and painted, too

hurt and angry to stay. Now, I'm back.
Our eyes home in on the bird's white

brow as she broods in a cupped
cavity, the only

markings in the precariously
balanced nest. A blur

of cinnamon and buff whizzes
overhead and drops

bugs into V-shaped
beaks. We think of them

as our chime
of wrens and monitor

chirps at feeding time as we mull
our months apart and joke about

how mad Mama Bird
must be at us for leaving the porch

light on or laughing
when she's trying to get

the babies to sleep so she
can frolic in the cottonwood

canopy, then disappear
into the living room

TV where you slouch on the love
seat and I collapse on the sofa

so our birds can rest. Daybreak,
you offer coffee with skim

milk while they've
vamoosed. No fallen

leaves, feathers, or tiny
bones, no signs

of foul play, as if they'd
followed a high note

into dogwoods—*tea
kettle, tea-kettle, tea-kettle,*

cheer—and soared
their separate ways.

Reliquary

Her father made a cedar hope chest for her trousseau.
Battered, scarred, now it is mine, a box to hold crazy
quilts, doilies, duvets, the tablecloth Great-Aunt
Gertrude crocheted—a thing too fancy for everyday:
pillowcases dotted with French knots, lazy
daisies, appliqués, and featherstitching on white
cotton, linen hand towels that say HIS or HERS.
A removable shelf perches on the rim, a tray
where she kept buttons in brown paper bags, pins,
needles, & thread to fix the fraying satin borders of
blankets. Do her soul and girlish dreams of
that tall man she'd meet and marry still float
on wind as a waxwing sings from the cedar's
branch? When I open the lid, fragrance of old
wood is like a lost tune I can't remember the
words to. I will live without her scent, her
lips on my cheek, the hesitant catch of her voice
when she can't recall words and I fill them in as if
we're identical twins and I'm finishing her sentences.
A mother's love never vanishes, fixed as
the North Star with no stops in a midnight sky.
Long ago, she gazed at the burled, aromatic
grain and vowed to keep all that survived its flames.

Midsummer

When you lost your wedding band
last winter, guessing it had slipped between

the driver's seat and door, you turned
the car upside-down and combed

the drive with a hand-held
torch. *A missing*

ring's not the most
favorable omen for a troubled

marriage, I muttered
when you phoned to deliver

the news. Days later, eating leftover
basmati rice, you found it

in the bowl. This late
midsummer afternoon you brought

a veggie sub home
as you do on Fridays. Opening

the bag, I found a black
velvet box that held

a diamond solitaire
set in palladium gold, so

loose I was afraid
I'd lose it. You took it back

but the resized
ring fell to the floor. Together

again after two seasons, did
my finger shrink in the lean

months apart? How do we find
the right fit—loose enough

to breathe but
snug enough to hold us?

Sweet Basil

grows bitter if you let it
go to seed, he said, so I'm careful

to pinch the buds instead of letting it
bloom as it did last summer

when he was my Facebook flame,
an Italian farmer flashing blue

eyes in a weathered
face. When he typed, *I*

love you more than my olive
groves and terraced

hills of grapevines, a green
spark shot up my spine. He meant it

only to tempt me
to talk dirty. *I'm*

launching a new
career writing erotica, I quipped,

but when I asked about his *famiglia,*
he shouted *Finito!* and our online fling

fizzled. Now I pick
tender leaves from basil

you planted and lay them
like petals on a linen

towel to dry
before dropping them

into the processor with extra
virgin olive oil—first

cold press—*pignola,*
garlic cloves and grated

parmesan. Tonight The Italian
Rapscallion appears

in my inbox after almost
a year—*Show me your*

boobs. I block
his messages and spoon

pesto over steaming
pasta for you, my husband, my heart. *It's*

the best I've ever tasted, you say, *so*
delicious and fresh.

Bone Moon

Swallow a tablet that tastes
like chalk. Chase it

with aspirin. Already
an inch

shorter than at 60, bones
thinner, body that

much closer to the grave, I almost
trip in the clearing where a bruised

moon looms above black branches. Can I
slip through these pines without

falling? Can my husband—no spring
chicken—catch me? Snow

crumbles under my skin
as the moon blooms only

to disappear
again.

Fallen Pearls

The string snapped on the *Fantasy*'s
emerald carpet when we cruised

between Charleston and Bermuda on a second
honeymoon. Restrung,

they glow
at my throat and possess

Mother's presence, her ghost. By the rough
rub against teeth, I can tell

they're real; they taste
of sea, salt, and sun. Seen

through a hand-held loupe, each
one's a blemished moon, blistered

and scarred. This fragile thread
binds them into a moment

forgotten but still connected
somewhere beyond winged

oysters and memories,
realigned.

Tombstone Bingo

We count cemeteries. First, a roadside
graveyard. *I hate those fake*

flowers, I scoff, *and those American
flags.* Then, I spot a headstone

display outside a monument
shop. *That's cheating,*

you say. *There could be
bodies under those stones,* I reply, so

grudgingly, you give me
half a point. As you drive,

I doze, then wake
to a sign for Bethlehem

Memorial Park and count it
although we can't see

mausoleums or angels, just
an arrow aimed at a narrow

lane. Miles
later, you spy lush

acres of lawn
that go on forever—the biggest

yet—and yell, *Cemetery!* but I'm
still ahead until

you count a single
tombstone on Route 52. *Cheater!*

I shout, but give
you credit because

who's to say one grave
isn't a graveyard? We pass a family

plot behind a wrought-iron
fence. *I should've seen*

that one coming since I pass it
twice a day, you sigh. We stop

keeping score, not
wanting to know who'll

be first to draw the last
breath, knowing no one wins

this contest.

Friends Post Photos of the Sky

Morning shots marbled copper
and cobalt, evening pearled

silver and mauve, thunder
storms, forked

lightning, the moon
in all its moods—musk

melon, milk-faced,
slightly askew. Years

ago, shoving a stroller
through snow, grocery

and diaper bags slung
over my shoulder—I looked up

as if from under water
at the sky's white-capped

waves, wondering if
there was a surface above

where I could breathe. Yesterday,
feeling sad, a friend

said, *Go outside
and look at the stars.* So

I stepped into silence, staring
up at lights pulsing

with the heat of a million
unanswered prayers.

Sandhills Gold

. . . in the Sandhills of North Carolina,
a few lucky beekeepers strike blue gold.
—Chick Jacobs

The year Daddy died, beekeepers found blue
honey in their hives. How it turns

blue or why it only happens
here no one knows. Some

think bees feed on bruised huckleberries, scuppernongs
or kudzu blossoms. Too far inland, Daddy

never found it in the forty-five years
he kept hives. In the nursing home, I talked

blue honey into blue eyes that
stared back in a blur

of lost memory and sleep. What
was he thinking? I spoke

of his veiled hat and long gloves,
bellowing hives

with smoke so he could pull combs and
honey from inside, and pour sourwood

into old Mason jars in slow motion
like the lengthening summer day

when the sky was so delphinium
it could be music, or the blue

shadow that followed me through the doorway
into the buzzing of bees when I

was thirteen, crying behind the pear tree because
I wasn't popular enough to be

May Queen. This is what I choose
to keep against forgetting:

You'll always
be my queen,

he said, bending
to kiss my forehead. I carry

that moment like a bee
in amber on a gold chain

above my heart to ward off wintering
broods and dark swarms, a queen without

a country or hive, standing in slanted light
as bees droned

around my head, weaving a crown of wings
and buzzing with sweetness.

    *****

Grief like honey left too long in the jar,
like the pint we bought last year

from a beekeeper who used to sell pot,
in the pantry all winter flanked by bottles

of blackstrap and Hungry Jack
crystallizing in the dark,

too solid to spoon onto bread unless you melt it
in water on the stove. Impatient,

I spread the gold grains on my toast, remembering
when he was alive and it

poured in slow
measures onto my mother's home-baked bread. One

summer he visited me in Chicago after robbing
his hive of a quart jar of sourwood, his

ankles so swollen
from stings he slept with his feet propped

on pillows. I want this
grief to dissolve like a lemon

lozenge on my tongue, I want
to taste the sweetness

of mornings
before sorrow, anger, and remorse

soured my vision of being
young and oblivious to his

pain, I want my words to flow
like a vein

onto the blue-lined page as holy
honey flowed from his white

hives onto our bread, our tongues, our lives.

About the Author

Beth Copeland
(author photo by Philip Rech)

The child of missionaries, Beth Copeland was born in Japan, where she spent her early childhood, as well as in India and the United States. Her first full-length poetry book *Traveling through Glass* received the 1999 Bright Hill Press Poetry Book Award. Her second book *Transcendental Telemarketer* was published by BlazeVOX in 2012. Her poems have appeared in literary journals and anthologies, including *Aeolian Harp*, *Atlanta Review*, *New Millennium Writings*, *The North American Review*, *Pedestal Magazine*, *Pirene's Fountain*, *Poet's Market*, *Rattle*, *The Southern Poetry Anthology*, and *Tar River Poetry* and have been featured on the PBS News Hour website. Beth received her MFA degree from Bowling Green State University in Ohio and teaches creative writing at her undergraduate alma mater, St. Andrews University. She lives with her husband Phil Rech and hound dog Kasey in a log cabin in North Carolina.

Previous Winners of The Dogfish Head Poetry Prize

2016 Mary B. Moore, *Flicker*
The Broadkill River Press, Milton, DE

2015 Faith Shearin, *Orpheus, Turning*
The Broadkill River Press, Milton, DE

2014 Lucian Mattison, *Peregrine Nation*
The Broadkill River Press, Milton, DE

2013 Grant Clauser, *Necessary Myths*
The Broadkill River Press, Milton, DE

2012 Tina Raye Dayton, *The Softened Ground*
The Broadkill Press, Milton, DE

2011 Sherry Gage Chappelle, *Salmagundi*
The Broadkill Press, Milton, DE

2010 Amanda Newell, *Fractured Light*
The Broadkill Press, Milton, DE

2009 David P. Kozinski, *Loopholes*
The Broadkill Press, Milton, DE

2008 Linda Blaskey, *Farm*
Bay Oak Publishers, Dover, DE

2007 Anne Agnes Colwell,
Father's Occupation, Mother's Maiden Name
Bay Oak Publishers, Dover, DE

2006 Scott Whitaker, *Field Recordings*
Bay Oak Publishers, Dover, DE

2005 Michael Blaine, *Murmur*
Bay Oak Publishers, Dover, DE

2004 Emily Lloyd, *The Most Daring of Transplants*
Argonne House Press, Washington, DC

2003 James Keegan *Of Fathers and Sons*
Argonne House Press, Washington, DC

Dogfish Head
Craft Brewed Ales

Dogfish Head is the first American craft brewery to focus on culinary-inspired beer recipes outside traditional beer styles and it has done so since the day it opened with the motto "off-centered ales for off-centered people." Since 1995, Dogfish has redefined craft beer and the way people think about beer by brewing with unique ingredients.

Today, Dogfish is among the fastest-growing breweries in the country and has won numerous awards throughout the years. Dogfish Head has grown into a 200+ person company with a restaurant/brewery/distillery in Rehoboth Beach, a beer-themed inn on the harbor in Lewes and a production brewery/distillery in Milton, Delaware.

Dogfish Head currently sells beer in 37 states and the District of Columbia, and is proud to sponsor The Dogfish Head Poetry prize, awarded now for fifteen consecutive years!

if a poet is
anybody,
he is somebody
to whom
things made
matter very little
...
somebody
who is
obsessed
by
Making.

- e.e. cummings

Other Titles from
The Broadkill River Press

Sounding the Atlantic   **Poetry by Martin Galvin**
ISBN 978-0-9826030-1-7 $14.95

That Deep & Steady Hum   **Poetry by Mary Ann Larkin**
ISBN 978-0-9826030-2-4 $14.95

Exile at Sarzanna   **Poetry by Laura Brylawski-Miller**
ISBN 978-0-9826030-5-5 $12.00

The Year of the Dog Throwers   **Poetry by Sid Gold**
ISBN 978-0-9826030-3-1 $12.00

Domain of the Lower Air   **Fiction by Maryanne Khan**
(National Book Critics Circle Award Nominee)
ISBN 978-0-9826030-4-8 $14.95

Speed Enforced by Aircraft   **Poetry by Richard Peabody**
(NBA Nominee, Pulitzer Prize Nominee)
ISBN 978-0-9826030-6-2 $15.95

Dutiful Heart   **Poetry by Joy Gaines-Friedler**
ISBN 978-1-940120-91-1 $16.00

Necessary Myths   **Poetry by Grant Clauser**
(Dogfish Head Poetry Prize Winner)
ISBN 978-1-940120-92-8 $14.95

Postcard from Bologna   **Poetry by Howard Gofreed**
(National Book Critics Circle Award Nominee)
ISBN 978-1-940-120-90-4 $15.95

Other Titles from
The Broadkill River Press

Lemon Light   Poetry by H. A. Maxson
    ISBN 978-1-940120-94-2 $15.95

Peregrine Nation   Poetry by Lucian Mattison
    (Dogfish Head Poetry Prize Winner)
    ISBN 978-1-940120-85-0 $15.95

On Gannon Street   Poetry by Mary Ann Larkin
    ISBN 978-1-940120-86-7 $12.00

The Table of the Elements   Poetry by J. T. Whitehead
    (National Book Award Nominee)
    ISBN 978-1-940120-93-5 $15.95

Good with Oranges   Poetry by Sid Gold
    (National Book Award Nominee)
    ISBN 978-1-940120-83-6 $16.00

Flicker   Poetry by Mary B. Moore
    (Dogfish Head Poetry Prize Winner)
    ISBN 978-1-940120-75-1 $16.95

Rock Taught   Poetry by David McAleavey
    (National Book Award Nominee)
    ISBN 978-1-940120-88-1 $16.95

Noise   Poetry by W. M. Rivera
    ISBN 978-1-940120-70-6 $16.95

Contents Under Pressure   Fiction by Ellen Prentiss Campbell
    (National Book Award Nominee)
    ISBN 978-1-940120-82-9 $16.95

The Broadkill Press The Key Poetry Series

(Series One)

The Black Narrows   **Poetry by S. Scott Whitaker**
ISBN 978-0-9837789-3-6 $9.95

Ice Solstice   **Poetry by Kelley Jean White**
ISBN 978-0-9837789-4-3 $8.95

Sediment and Other Poems   **Poetry by Gary Hanna**
ISBN 978-0-9837789-5-0 $9.95

Sound Effects   **Poetry by Nina Bennett**
ISBN 978-0-9837789-6-7 $8.95

Taken Away   **Poetry by Carolyn Cecil**
ISBN 978-0-9837789-7-4 $8.95

Where Night Comes From   **Poetry by Shea Garvin**
ISBN 978-0-9837789-8-1 $10.95

(Series Two)

charmed life   **Poetry by Buck Downs**
ISBN # 978-1-940120-96-6 $10.95

The Stories We Tell   **Poetry by Irene Fick**
ISBN # 978-1-940120-98-0 $9.95

Brackish Water   **Poetry by Michael Blaine**
ISBN # 978-1-940120-99-7 $10.95

Love, War and Music   **Poetry by Franetta McMillian**
ISBN # 978-1-940120-89-8 $9.95

Highway 78   **Poetry by Susanne Bostick Allen**
ISBN 978-1-940120-80-5 $9.95

FLUX Quanta   **Poetry by James Michael Robbins**
ISBN 978-1-940120-81-2 $10.95

The Broadkill Press The Key Poetry Series

The Key Poetry Series
(Series Three)

Silence, Interrupted   Poetry by Jim Bourey
(Winner 2016 Best Book of Verse, Delaware Press Association)
ISBN 978-1-940120-87-4 $9.95

Matchstick & Bramble   Poetry by Lucy Simpson
ISBN 978-1-940120-87-4 $9.95

Gridley Park (forthcoming)   Poetry by Ronald Wilson
ISBN 978-1-940120-71-3 $10.95

"Purple, Purple" (forthcoming)   Poetry by Ian Walton
ISBN 978-1-940120-72-0 $12.95

Other Chapbooks from The Broadkill Press

Loopholes   Poetry by David P. Kozinski
2009 Dogfish Head Poetry Prize Winner
ISBN 978-0-9826030-0-0 $7.00

Fractured Light   Poetry by Amanda Newell
2010 Dogfish Head Poetry Prize Winner
ISBN 978-0-9826030-7-9 $7.95

Salmagundi   Poetry by Sherry Gage Chappelle
2011 Dogfish Head Poetry Prize Winner
ISBN 978-0-9826030-9-3 $9.00

Other Chapbooks from
The Broadkill Press

The Softened Ground   Poetry by Tina Raye Dayton
     2012 Dogfish Head Poetry Prize Winner
     ISBN 978-0-9837789-0-5 $9.00

Constructing Fiction   Essays on Craft by Jamie Brown
     ISBN 978-0-9826030-8-6 $6.00

L'Heure bleu   Meta-Fiction by David R. Slavitt
     ISBN 978-0-9837789-1-2 $11.95

The Homestead Poems   Poetry by Gary Hanna
Honoring the 75th Anniversary of The Rehoboth Art League
     ISBN 978-0-9837789-2-9 $10.95

Sakura: A Cycle of Haiku   Poetry by Jamie Brown
(Winner 2013 Best Book of Verse, Delaware Press Association)
     ISBN 978-0-9837789-9-8 $10.95